8/07

To Dad,

We found this book in the Gift Shop at the 72nd or the Public Library on the 42nd Street. We thought of you & Mom immediately. Maybe you'll even see someone you know in the pictures!

Enjoy & Happy Birthday!

With love,
Rich, Lori, Matthew & Julie

D1288449

Life on the Lower East Side

"People ask me—how did you know what to take? I didn't even have to think. I just went outside, and there were the streets of my mother, of me, and whatnot. Very alive, full of activity, with people."

Life on the Lower East Side

Photographs by Rebecca Lepkoff,

1937–1950

Text by Peter E. Dans and Suzanne Wasserman

Princeton Architectural Press, New York

Published by
Princeton Architectural Press
37 East Seventh Street
New York, New York 10003

For a free catalog of books, call 1.800.722.6657.
Visit our web site at www.papress.com.

Frontispiece: "Stoop of 343 Cherry Street"
Page 13: "No Rooms. Janitor in Store."

Editing: Linda Lee
Design: Jan Haux

Special thanks to: Nettie Aljian, Dorothy Ball, Nicola Bednarek, Janet
Behning, Becca Casbon, Penny (Yuen Pik) Chu, Russell Fernandez, Pete
Fitzpatrick, Clare Jacobson, John King, Mark Lamster, Nancy Eklund
Later, Katharine Myers, Lauren Nelson, Scott Tennent, Jennifer Thompson,
Paul Wagner, Joseph Weston, and Deb Wood of Princeton Architectural
Press —Kevin C. Lippert, publisher

Library of Congress Cataloging-in-Publication Data

Lepkoff, Rebecca.
    Life on the Lower East Side / photographs by Rebecca Lepkoff,
  1937/1950 ; text by Peter E. Dans and Suzanne Wasserman.
        p.   cm.
    Includes bibliographical references.
    ISBN-13: 978-1-56898-606-7 (hardcover : alk. paper)
    1. Lower East Side (New York, N.Y.)—Social life and customs—20th
  century—Pictorial works. 2. New York (N.Y.)—Social life and customs
  —20th century—Pictorial works. 3. City and town life—New York (State)
  —New York—History—20th century—Pictorial works. 4. Street life
  —New York (State)—New York—History—20th century—Pictorial works.
  I. Dans, Peter E. II. Wasserman, Suzanne. III. Title.
  F128.68.L6L46 2006
  779'.997471—dc22

                                                          2006000636

Table of Contents

Acknowledgments

I am thankful to Howard Greenberg of The Howard Greenberg Gallery in New York City for recognizing the beauty and value of my photographs and displaying them on his walls. The complete collection of my photographs, including those of the Lower East Side presented in this book, is now housed at his gallery. I am grateful to Ann Wilkes Tucker, curator of photography at The Museum of Fine Arts, Houston, Texas, who gathered The Photo League's work into a stunning exhibit, which included my photographs from 1930 to 1940, at The International Center of Photography (ICP) in 1978. This show stirred the artistic world and brought collectors running. I am also indebted to Susan Fleminger of the Henry Street Settlement House who showed my Lower East Side photographs from the 1940s at the exhibit titled The Lower East Side (1984) at the Abrons Arts for Living Center in the Lower East Side. People of the neighborhood recognized their fathers and grandmothers in the photographs and were reminded of the stories by the elders told of life then.

I would like to thank the Stephen Daiter Gallery in Chicago, in collaboration with John Cleary Gallery, Houston, Texas, for publishing of the book This was the Photo League (2001) and for a one-woman show of my work, Essaying the Neighborhood (Lower East Side 1940–50) (2002). I would like to recognize Walter Rosenblum, president of The Photo League, whose spirit and energy kept the organization alive; friends I met at the Photo League: Rosalie Gwathmey, Arthur Leipzig, Morris Huberland, Morris Engel, and Nina and Naomi Rosenblum; Michael Spano, for the exhibit at the Fourteenth Street YMHA NYC (1983); and David Godlis, Sy Rubin, David Channon, Nell Blaine, Martha Hurt Loewy, Marilyn Reynolds, Peggy Wreen, Jana Haimsohn, Richard Reich, Vince Ciani, John Goodman, Jana Haimsohn, Steve Zeitlin, and Marci Reaven. These artists, teachers, and curators touched my life and work with their gifts of intuition and knowledge.

I am grateful to Arnold Eagle, my first teacher and friend, who also loved the people and streets of the Lower East Side and remembered my early training in modern dance that tuned me into the choreography of the movement of the streets; to Sid Grossman, a gutsy inspirational teacher who critiqued my work and taught me to print beautiful photographs; and to my dear family, who encouraged my efforts and dealt with the cumbersome arrangement of having a darkroom in the apartment.

My admiration goes out to Peter Dans, whose dream of a book of his boyhood life on the Lower East Side led him on a magical, admirable journey from the Lower East Side Tenement Museum to Suzanne Wasserman, of the Gotham Center for New York City History at CUNY, to myself. He fell in love with a great stack of my photographs of the Lower East Side taken between 1940 and 1950. His search finally led to Nancy Eklund Later and Linda Lee of Princeton Architectural Press, where my images were visualized into this book. Without the initiative and energy of Peter Dans and Suzanne Wasserman, this book would not have been realized. I thank them and all the people involved in making this book possible.

—Rebecca Lepkoff

I dedicate this book to the memory of my beloved wife,
Colette; my parents, Filomena and Emanuel Dans; my grandmother
Catherine Lisanti; and my uncles, Peter and John Lisanti.
I am grateful to Suzanne Dans, Janet Worthington, Pamela
Thomas, and Linda Lee for their invaluable assistance in
helping develop and edit my chapter and to Eric Robinson of
the New York Historical Society Library, David Smith of the
New York Public Library, Ken Cobb, Director of the New York
City Department of Records/Municipal Archives, Mary Brown,
and Father John Nobiletti for research assistance. I am also
very grateful to Ollie Owen, Bill Roberts, Blair Worthington,
Don and Nancy Reynolds, Peter Quinn, and the late Jim Shenton
for their encouragement when this book seemed to be an
impossible dream. That dream became a reality when someone at
the Lower East Side Tenement Museum referred me to Suzanne
Wasserman. She told me about Rebecca Lepkoff's treasure
trove of photos from the old neighborhood and a friendly and
productive collaboration was born. The final piece fell into
place when agent John Thornton said he could not take me on
but recognized the project's potential and gave me a list of
seven publishers to contact with Princeton Architectural Press
at the top. A Friday afternoon telephone call led me to Nancy
Eklund Later who shared our excitement and helped champion the
book into existence.

—Peter E. Dans

I dedicate this book to my family: David and Raphael Stern;
my mother, Eileen Wasserman; my sisters, Tina, Stephanie,
and Nadine; and to the memory of my father, Dr. Edward M.
Wasserman and to my mentors, Judith Stein, my senior English
teacher at Kenwood High School on the South Side of Chicago,
and Daniel T. Rodgers of Princeton University, who was my
professor and advisor at the University of Wisconsin, Madison.
When I moved to New York City in 1980, I became fascinated

by the Lower East Side and its hold on the historical imagination of New Yorkers and Americans. In 1990, I finished a dissertation that looked at the Lower East Side between the wars and its role in shaping American Jewish nostalgia and memory. Soon after, Susan Fleminger of Henry Street Settlement introduced me to Rebecca Lepkoff. Her photographs covered the exact time period of my work. I fell in love with her work, and she became a wonderful friend—the kind of creative, warm, and intelligent woman I had always imagined flourished in New York City. I want to thank the historian Mike Wallace for his ongoing support—in every way. I am grateful to Nancy Eklund Later for recognizing the importance of this project when it was in its nascence and to Linda Lee for her dedication, insight, and commitment to this book.

—Suzanne Wasserman

"Mothers with children. People would hang out of the windows and talk from the windows. They would sit outside and clean the windows. You'd get photographs of that. Or they'd sit on the fire escape when it was hot, and they'd sit on the stoops and talk."

Union
Square

Houston Street

Bowery

Delancey Street

East Broadway

Canal Street

Centre Street

City Hall
Park

Manhattan Bridge

Fulton Street

Brooklyn Bridge

Battery
Park

The
Aquarium

Map of the Lower East
Side, ca. 1939. Drawing
by Matt Knutzen.
Basemap courtesy of the City of
New York.

There Once Was A Neighborhood

By Peter E. Dans

I'm a New Yorker. Forget the fact that I haven't lived there
for over forty years. My accent and rate of speech betray me.
I'm the living embodiment of the old adage, "You can take
the boy out of New York, but you can't take New York out of
the boy." Paradoxically, though, you can take New York out
of New York.

In *The Colossus of New York*, Colson Whitehead says we
create our own personal New York, and when part of it
disappears, what was there before becomes "more real and
solid than what is there now." My New York is the Lower East
Side, not the storied portion designated on the U.S. Register
of Historic Places, but a forgotten area bounded by the
Brooklyn and Manhattan bridges, the East River, and the Third
Avenue elevated line along the Bowery and Pearl Street.
That neighborhood, which was demolished in 1950 to build the
Alfred E. Smith housing project, remains very real to me.

Its polyglot character was the legacy of two centuries
of continuity and change. During colonial times, Cherry
Street was the fashionable home of wealthy Dutch and English
merchants, shipbuilders, and lawyers. After his first
inauguration, George Washington lived at One Cherry Street,
commemorated by a plaque on a nearby Brooklyn Bridge stanchion
obscured now by a fence and debris. The residence, later a
piano store, was torn down in 1856 to build shops. Brooks
Brothers and Lord & Taylor started serving the carriage trade
on Catherine Street before following their clients uptown in
the 1830s.

The area then became the first stop for Irish, German,
Italian, Polish, Spanish, Portuguese, Greek, Jewish, and
Chinese immigrants as well as African-Americans and Puerto
Ricans, all seeking a better life. They worked in the hide,
glue, and leather factories on Frankfort and William streets,
Harper Brothers Publishers on Franklin Square, the Journal
American newspaper plant on South Street, the Fulton Fish

Author's neighborhood
on the Lower East
Side as seen from
Brooklyn, 1938.
Detail of "Brooklyn
Bridge and City
Skyline 1938."
Copyright Corbis/Bettman
Archive.

The Alfred E. Smith
Housing Project,
the banal build-
ings and highway
extension that re-
placed the author's
lively neighbor-
hood, as seen from
the Brooklyn Bridge
in 1974. Also in
the photograph
are Knickerbocker
Village and the old
Journal American
newspaper plant.
Photograph by Edmund V.
Gillon, Jr.

market, on ferries, in freight terminals, and as seamen, chandlers, corders, coopers, and wainers, serving the maritime industry through which New York gained world prominence.

From the 1850s through the 1920s, it was a rough neighborhood, as attested to by the numerous missions aimed at saving the souls of its inhabitants, especially sailors, prostitutes, and alcoholics. One ominous sign read, "Be Sure Your Sin Will Find You Out." It was home to Boss Tweed, Tammany Hall, Al Smith, and the heavily Irish Fourth Ward. By 1937, when I was born, it had become predominantly Italian and relatively stable with a low crime rate. It was very much like the countless neighborhoods that E. B. White described in his 1947 essay "Here is New York," a "city within a city... virtually self-sufficient [and usually] no more than two or three blocks long and a couple of blocks wide." He noted that New Yorkers had such a strong sense of place that they considered moving three blocks as "moving away." So it was for my family.

Lower East Side Roots

Author's mother holding author at age three months under the Manhattan Bridge, 1937
Courtesy of author

My grandmother, Caterina Virelli, came to the United States from Ferrandina, Italy at age nine after her father's death in 1904. She attended P.S.1, as had Jimmy Durante and Eddie Cantor. Despite having to drop out after the fifth grade to do piecework at home, she always championed the value of education. At sixteen, she married Joseph Lisanti who had also immigrated from Ferrandina. They moved into 344 Water Street (344) where they had three children: Peter, Johnny, who became mentally disabled at age three after a bout of meningitis, and Filomena, my mother. A beautiful woman, she caught the eye of a nearby paper-stock owner twice her age and, in 1936, dropped out of Hunter College at eighteen to marry him, against the wishes of both families. After an unusually lavish reception for the time, they moved into an apartment on 40 Monroe Street, part of Knickerbocker Village, an upscale apartment complex built in 1934 as part of plan designed to replace the tenements with housing for white-collar workers in the Financial District.

When I was eight months old, my father abandoned us, and two months later, we were evicted for not paying the rent. Embarrassed and distraught, my mother moved in with her maid of honor's family on Staten Island. Apparently, my mother considered putting me up for adoption (common during the Depression), but my grandmother forbade it. My mother and I then moved into the vacant third floor apartment in 344, and my grandmother, whom I called Nonny, cared for me while my mother worked as a bank teller at Irving Trust and as a dental assistant at New York University and completed night school at Hunter College.

In 1943, after five years of legal wrangling, my mother won a contested divorce and married Emanuel Dans (Dad), a Spaniard whom she met through his aged mother who lived on the first floor of 344. Dad had entered my life two years earlier, and it was not until my teens, when I was asked to consent to an adoption, that I found out that he was not my biological father. Dad's early life is shrouded in mystery. He spent his early childhood near La Coruna, Spain, and, after returning to the U.S., shipped out as a stoker to Shanghai, China, and Vladivostok, Russia, at fifteen, possibly after a shooting at his father's bar. He was a union activist, participating in a march on Washington, and also fought briefly in the Spanish Civil War.

I do know that he spent over half of World War II as a Merchant Marine on various ships ferrying troops and supplies to Murmansk, Russia, in the North Atlantic; Casablanca, Morocco; Anzio, Italy; and New Guinea. For some time after the war, he woke up in terror, dreaming of submarine alerts. After the war, he bought the Blue Marlin restaurant in a remote area of Staten Island in anticipation of the Verrazano Bridge that was not built for twenty years. The only steady customers were children from a nearby orphanage whom he rarely charged. The restaurant failed, and he went back to sea as a marine engineer on Grace Line cruises to the Caribbean and South America. He always returned loaded with presents: comic books, a canary, a troupial (a South American oriole with a piercing whistle), goldfish, a puppy, a bunny, and even a duck. The latter three had a very short tenure in our apartment.

344 Water Street

A three-story brick building with a Dutch blue wooden door , 344 can be traced back at least to 1810 when David Keeler, a self-described "hatter," lived there. During my time, it sat between a Spanish-American Café and a hand laundry and housed three cold-water flats, so named because they had no hot running water. The apartments were arranged like railroad cars with the kitchen, bedroom, and living room lined up in a row, with two side bedrooms at each end. The toilet was on the landing. The apartment's major source of warmth was the wood stove in the kitchen, where water was heated for the weekly tub bath. The bedroom farthest from the wood stove was called the cold room. To take the chill out in the winter, Nonny used a kerosene heater. She also heated bricks on the stove, wrapped them in flannel, and put them under the bedcovers to warm the sheets.

Author's home at 344 Water Street, ca. 1939, with Uncle Johnny looking out the window. Municipal Archives tax photo. Courtesy of NYC Municipal Archives.

The most memorable feature of 344 was its large third-floor landing with an enormous skylight that lit up the stairwells. A fire escape led to the tar-lined roof, which was a great place to escape the heat and to view Brooklyn and the bridges across the East River.

Life in a Cold-water Flat

Lower East Siders traditionally greeted visitors saying, "Sit, eat something." To set a good table, they had to be creative because of low income, food scarcity, and a lack of appliances for storage or cooking. Before widespread refrigeration, fresh fruits and vegetables were only available in summer from

horse-drawn carts or pushcarts. Butter, eggs, and cheese, now
in every grocery store dairy case, were sold by the "Butter
and Egg men" in special stores like Hearn's on Fulton Street.
In the absence of refrigerators, food was kept fresh and
safe in the icebox, a wooden or enameled cabinet with a top
compartment for perishables and a bottom for large blocks of
ice. Underneath the icebox sat a basin to collect the melting
ice. The icebox was regularly stocked by icemen, immigrants
from Bari, Italy. Relatively short in stature, they seemed
like supermen, lugging a big wooden bucket
with a large block of ice along with a can of
kerosene up two flights of stairs. I loved to
watch them chip the ice and then use their
ice pick and tongs to break off just the
right size block.

During World War II, each family got a
limited number of ration stamps for food,
which had to be carefully stored from rats,
roaches, and other insects. The vacuum seals
of cans were checked regularly to avoid
botulism. Our cans also served as game pieces
in "grocery store," a game that I played with
my great-grandmother, Gee-Gee, who spoke only
Italian. She played the storekeeper, and I
purchased the cans using pieces of paper bags
as currency. This game and the Italian card
games *scopa* and *briscola* are responsible for
my rudimentary Italian.

My memories of meals revolve around
my grandfather, who moved freight with a
handcart, known as "pushing the truck," at the Pennsylvania
Railroad terminal under the Brooklyn Bridge. Like other
railroad workers, he had a strict sense of time. At six
o'clock, he would pull out his pocket watch and expect
everyone to be sitting down for dinner. Latecomers were
threatened with the leather strop he used for sharpening his
straight razor. At his feet was a carefully guarded gallon

A Four Generations
photograph taken in a
Battery Park visit to the
Aquarium showing Gee-Gee,
Nonny, author's mother,
and author
Courtesy of author

The Pennsylvania Railroad Terminal under the Brooklyn Bridge at South Street where author's grandfather worked "pushing the truck" in the 1940s.

of Petri or Gallo wine, which we called "under-the-table" wine. Dinners followed a regular pattern. On Tuesdays and Fridays, we would have fish, usually whiting or mackerel from the Fulton Fish Market. On Wednesday and Sundays, we had macaroni with gravy. On Mondays and Thursdays, we ate *pastafazoola*, minestrone, or *Caldo Gallego* (Spanish soup). On Saturdays, we might splurge and have chicken or calf's liver and onions.

Special foods that could not be cooked on a wood-burning stove, such as lasagna, Thanksgiving turkey, and Easter braided bread with whole eggs in the crust, were prepared at home and taken to a privately owned *fornaio* (oven) for baking. The fornaio's specialty was *capuzelle*, roasted sheep's head. Though I remember liking it, I did not relish eating the brains, which were reputed to make one smarter. The store next door to the fornaio sold *scungilli* (eels), which I could never bring myself to eat. My idea of a delicacy was a gigantic crumb bun we got each Sunday from Larry's pastry shop on Roosevelt Street, as well as *sfogliatelle* (a pastry), *cannolis*, and lemon ice from Savoia's on Catherine Street,

During this era, neighborhood residents rarely ate out. My first restaurant meal was steak at the Log Cabin Restaurant on Pearl Street when I turned eleven. Later birthdays were celebrated with a sizzling swordfish steak and Nesselrode pie at Sweet's restaurant on Fulton Street, the descendant of a refectory opened by Abraham Sweet, a victualler, in 1847. Sweet's was a magnet for celebrities, sports stars, and aficionados of seafood. They took no reservations, and the lines, especially on Fridays, stretched down the stairs of the second floor restaurant and on to Fulton Street. Sweet's was known for excellent service by knowledgeable waiters, one of whom was in his nineties, and all of whom remembered what regulars liked to order.

During summertime, to escape the stifling heat, we would pack fried eggplant sandwiches and take the Culver Line to the beach at Coney Island and, before returning, make a stop at Steeplechase. Some Sundays, we would walk to the aquarium in Battery Park, which Robert Moses vindictively shut down in 1942 and later demolished after FDR blocked his plan to build a bridge from the Battery to Brooklyn. Another favorite destination was City Hall Park, where after feeding the pigeons and having a Foremost ice cream pop, we would visit Frederick William MacMonnies' wonderful statue of Nathan Hale and read the inscription. My mother and I would also sometimes go to the air-conditioned Tribune Theater on Printer's Square (now Pace College) where my life-long fascination with the movies began.

Mom, Dad, and School Days

I was fortunate that before my mother and I were evicted from Knickerbocker Village, a well-known pediatrician, Dr. Mary Walsh, lived in our apartment building. Until she moved uptown in 1942, Dr. Walsh saw me regularly and wrote forty pages of meticulous instructions and diagrams, which my mother kept with other records of the period hidden under her bed until she died in 1991. When Dr. Walsh discharged me, her notes contained suggestions for continuing medical care, free recreation facilities, and potential schools.

In 1941, my mother used a ten-dollar-a-week child-care allowance to send me to kindergarten at St. John's Villa Academy, a boarding school run by the Congregation of the Sisters of Saint John the Baptist on Staten Island. I remember very little from the period except that it entailed a ferry-boat ride and a train trip in the dark on Sundays. One happy consequence of writing this memoir was reconnecting with my first grade teacher Sister Ermelinda who still teaches there at age ninety-one. She picked me out of a first grade photograph and told me where I sat and that I was a quiet student.

In 1944, my mother began working as an Italian and Spanish interpreter at the Criminal Courts building and enrolled me in the third grade, under a completely new name, at nearby Transfiguration parish on Mott Street. To illustrate the power of the mind, I never remember being called by my original name. Transfiguration was a perfect embodiment of a diverse and changing New York, having begun life in 1827 in a former Episcopal Church on Ann Street and, eight years later, moving to a former Dutch Reformed Presbyterian Church on Chambers Street. The pastor Felix Varela was an immigrant who had been a Cuban representative to the Spanish parliament but became persona non grata for advocating Cuban independence from Spain and the abolition of slavery there. In 1853, the congregation moved to the present building, built in 1801 by Dutch Lutherans who later converted en masse to Episcopalianism. Staffed by immigrant priests from Ireland, Poland, Italy, Portugal, and Turkey, it served what was then an Irish and German enclave. By the early 1900s, the Salesian nuns were brought in to teach the predominantly Italian student population. After World War II, with the increase in Chinese students, the Salesian nuns were replaced by Maryknoll nuns who had been driven out of Mainland China.

Uncle Vito's barbershop next to exit from the El at Chatham Square. Note the cost of haircut and shave.

Each morning, my mother walked me to school, using the Third Avenue El station to cross over sprawling Chatham Square. We would then pass the barbershop where my great-uncle Vito specialized in using leeches to treat "shiners," or black eyes. During inclement weather, I would wait for my mother in the convent on Park (now Mosco) Street. On nice days, I would play "skelly" (a game in which a weighted soda cap was navigated around a board drawn with chalk), punchball, stoopball, and marbles in Columbus Park, once the site of Mulberry Bend and Five Points, notorious nineteenth-century slums.

In 1947, I entered a combined sixth- and-seventh-grade class taught by Sister Mary Berchmans Flynn, a Maryknoll nun, who decided to skip me a grade, which entailed moving my seat one row over. She told my parents that the school could not meet my needs and that she was afraid I would get picked on because I was much younger and smaller than my classmates. After I was pummeled by two boys, Dad bought me boxing gloves and a punching bag, but I never became much of a fighter.

Dad had always wanted to attend a military academy so I applied to La Salle Military Academy in Oakdale, Long Island. Situated on a magnificent property on the Great South Bay, La Salle was like entering another world. After completing the eighth grade, I was declared ineligible to compete for the one high school scholarship, which was restricted to residents of Queens County. My mother reacted angrily and suggested I be withdrawn. Instead, Dad decided to ship out on six-week rather than two-week cruises in order to cover the tuition and board, which came to a hefty $1,500, not including books, incidentals, and periodic travel home on the Long Island Railroad. Despite being ashore less, Dad never complained and made sure he was home for special events. Both were proud when I was named the outstanding graduating senior.

Nonny and Lessons in Kindness

Because my parents were often gone during my early years, most of my 344 memories revolve around Nonny, the family's heart and soul. Nonny worked weekends as a cleaning woman at the Hotel Pierre, using the extra money for private doctors in an unsuccessful attempt to cure Uncle Johnny's muteness and disability. Between her work and keeping house for her busy family, Nonny could not watch over him as he grew into a strapping but defenseless young man. In 1940, Nonny reluctantly agreed to place him, at age twenty, in the Wassaic State School, an outstanding mental health institution in rural Dutchess County, where he still lives at eighty-six—a tribute to his strong constitution and the excellent caregivers.

Every other Saturday, rain or shine, Nonny traveled one hundred miles by subway and train to Wassaic and up a steep

Nonny with a pack on her back carrying special treats to Uncle Johnny at Wassaic State School, 1948
Courtesy of author

The Columbus Day Parade in 1947. Nonny at center in Italian peasant dress with castanets in one hand and the American and Italian flags in the other. The author, age ten, in the front carrying the American flag.

Courtesy of author

hill to Uncle Johnny's building carrying a backpack loaded with treats. On my visits, I was startled by the long lines of developmentally disabled boys and men in one section, and girls and women in the other. They made faces, yelled out, and waved as they walked or were wheeled from building to building. My first impulse was to look away, but Nonny gently told me that they craved attention and affection and suggested I smile, wave back, and speak a kind word. In so doing, she taught me to see humanity in the unfamiliar and to turn fear and aversion into compassion.

During the war, Nonny began as a cleaning woman on the four-to-midnight shift at the Brooklyn Borough Hall while managing a busy household. When Gee-Gee became bed-ridden from a devastating stroke, she lovingly cleaned, bathed, turned, and fed her for a year until her death in 1946 at ninety-six. Gee-Gee's body was prepared in the house by the Vanellas, who ran the funeral parlor on Madison Street. She was left in her own bed for the wake while family and friends paid their respects.

The visits to Uncle Johnny and watching Nonny nursing Gee-Gee left a deep impression and likely affected my decision to become a doctor, as did the altruism that was her hallmark. One example was her practice of sending money and packages to "adopted" children in Italian orphanages and to starving Europeans. One day while helping her carry packages to the post office on Pine Street about fifteen blocks away, I asked her why we were doing this. She answered, "Because the people are poor." I replied that we were poor too. She agreed, but said that they were poorer and that we were lucky because we lived in America. Indeed, she was equally proud of her American citizenship and her Italian heritage. For many years, she led the Department of Public Works down Fifth Avenue in the Columbus Day Parade.

Nonny also played a role in one of my last and most vivid memories of 344, the blizzard of 1947, which paralyzed New York City. Fortunately, we had stocked up enough food, wood, and kerosene for the Christmas holidays, so we were able to sit inside and enjoy watching the snow fall. The task of shoveling the snow in the aftermath was formidable. Nonny and I took short breaks to throw snowballs at one another and to sing Christmas carols. When all the shoveling was done, I remember that the walls of the path towered over me. For a while, we sat at the front door in the light of the old Bishop's crook lamppost, basking in the peace and serenity of the deserted street. Since then, I've always appreciated such quiet moments spent with loved ones.

Uncle Pete standing at the far right in his policeman's uniform at a ribbon-cutting for the opening of the Brooklyn Battery Tunnel May 25, 1950. Among the dignitaries are Mayor William O'Dwyer (cutting the ribbon) and next to him from right to left: Parks Commissioner Robert Moses, Manhattan Borough President Robert Wagner, Archbishop of New York Francis Cardinal Spellman, Brooklyn Borough President John Cashmore, and City Council President Vincent Impelliteri.
Courtesy of photographer Bill Wallace/New York Daily News.

Uncle Pete and Having Fun

In Dad's absence, Uncle Pete was both a father figure and a big brother. He had dropped out of Brooklyn Polytechnic High School to work in the Fulton Fish Market. Not drafted because of a "spot on his lung," he served as a fireman at First Army headquarters on Governor's Island. Later, he worked as a

milkman, a policeman at the Brooklyn Battery Tunnel, a toll
collector on the Henry Hudson Parkway, and an inspector of
weights and measures at Hunt's Point Market.

Uncle Pete was a happy-go-lucky and generous man, quick to
please. That same impulsiveness and openness would often get
him into trouble as he said whatever came into his head—wise or
unwise. He was great at coining words and passing on unusual
ones, which remain his most enduring legacy. Whenever he wanted
me to disappear, he would tell me "to randifulate," "scram-
ammy," or "hit the road." He was a great tease and, instead of
my first name, which had been unofficially changed to his, he
called me various names such as "mahoska," "chuche" (Italian
dialect for donkey), "hoople" (after the clueless cartoon
character "Major Hoople"), and "chiacchiarone" (Italian for
chatterbox). These terms were used affectionately, sometimes
for a perceived inadequacy, but often to get a rise from my
mother, who invariably took the bait.

His major obsessions were gambling and fixing cars.
He pored over the racing form and always had a new system
but was too impatient to pocket even winnings of hundreds
of dollars, wanting to parlay them into a "big killing."
Afterward, he would use some convoluted logic to explain how
he had lost, but "still came out ahead." He always seemed to
be driving some unsafe jalopy like his 1933 Pontiac with its
missing floorboards. They had doors that had to be tied shut
or car starters that needed rigging and which he activated by
jiggling something under the dashboard. He worked on them with
a jumble of tools and old parts that he picked up from various
junkyards.

On lazy summer Sunday afternoons when the downtown
workers were gone, he and I would play softball on a deserted
Burling Slip, now part of the South Street marketplace.
His biggest treats were taking me to the "nosebleed seats"
in the end arena of the old Madison Square Garden where I
succumbed to the curse of being a life-long New York Rangers
fan. At home, we would improvise a hockey game with rolled-
up stockings or a rubber ball known as a "Spaldeen." Most

afternoons we listened to the radio, starting with the racing results and then *The Shadow*, *The Green Hornet*, *The Lone Ranger*, and *Captain Midnight*, whose decoder badge was a prized possession. Along with information about the bad guys, I was regularly reminded to drink my Ovaltine.

On rainy days, Uncle Pete would play 78 rpm records on the Victrola, singing and dancing with a battered top hat along with his favorites who naturally became mine: Fred Astaire; Cab Calloway; The Ink Spots; and Ted Lewis, whose signature line was "Is everybody happy?" and who, as Doctor Lewis, dispensed "Homemade Sunshine," consisting of "a song, a little hope, love, laughter, and a kind word."

Uncle Pete was what used to be called "a gay blade." Nicknamed "Rudy" because of his resemblance to the silent movie heartthrob Rudolph Valentino, he was a regular patron at Roseland Ballroom where he met his wife. A hastily arranged marriage in 1948 ended in divorce years later. He was sui generis in the true sense of the term. Only he would cancel a doctor's appointment because he wasn't feeling well, as he did on the day of his death. The week before, he had canceled a long-planned evaluation for surgery on a large abdominal aneurysm. His reason? He had been given a free coupon for a trip to Atlantic City, and it was only good for that day. Fittingly, he won seventy dollars and went out a winner on his own terms, dying in his sleep—something for which many eighty year olds devoutly wish. One of his last requests was that his dancing shoes be placed in his casket, because he planned to "dance with the angels." When told that they might not be dancers, he said that he would teach them. He was a constant source of affection, admiration, and bonhomie. He enriched my life, teaching me how to lighten up as well as how to avoid the mistakes he has made.

The Razing of 344

We had no desire to leave 344, which had been our family's home for four decades through four generations. However, in 1948, 344 was razed, ironically as was Al Smith's birthplace

The International Bar, a Greek cafe and the stoop of the apartment building at 40-44 Madison Street where author and his family were "relocated" in 1948.

at 174 South Street, to build the first phase of the housing project bearing Smith's name. Having survived almost two centuries, 344 did not go down easily. Our family, among the last to be evicted, was "relocated" by the city to temporary residence in two apartments at 42 Madison Street. Dating from at least 1811, it had been modernized and enlarged from two to six stories. Our apartment, with its indoor toilet and bathtub in the kitchen, sat above a Greek cafe from which the sounds of music and dancing could be heard well past midnight on weekends. Although 42 Madison rivaled many buildings that today command high rents on the Upper West Side, it was destroyed in 1950 to complete the housing project.

Neither of our families had incomes low enough to qualify for the Smith project; so my grandparents were relocated to the Vladeck project at 636 Water Street and my parents and I to the Dyckman project in Inwood, two hundred blocks uptown. Given our family's closeness, the separation was emotionally difficult. The move meant long commutes to my mother's work at 100 Centre Street and my father's Union Hall on Maiden Lane and the piers downtown. More importantly, the distance severely restricted the time we could spend with Nonny who was fiercely independent. After my grandfather died, Nonny refused to move when my parents were able to afford a home of their own in the Bronx in the 1960s, preferring to remain on the Lower East Side until she suffered a stroke at age ninety-four.

My extended family was part of Robert Moses's controlled diaspora of diverse communities in the 1940s and 1950s. In the first phase of the Smith Project, Moses replaced a neighborhood of seventeen hundred people living in sturdy low-rise brick housing that harked back to the area's seafaring, colonial, and immigrant past with an enclave of banal high-rise buildings accommodating only two hundred more people, few of whom were among those dispossessed. Like his other housing projects, it lacked cross streets and stores, isolating the inhabitants from one another and the surrounding community. This sense of isolation was compounded by the creation of spaghettilike vehicular overpasses on the project's east and south sides.

Frances Perkins, FDR's Secretary of Labor, once said that Moses "loved the public, but not as people." To him, we were slum dwellers to be moved around like pawns on a chessboard. Unlike E. B. White, Moses failed to appreciate the importance of neighborhoods. He saw them as clusters of buildings, rather than as living, breathing organisms populated by people interacting with and serving one another. Although gritty, they are also fragile, and when they disappear, they cannot be easily re-created.

Through Rebecca Lepkoff's pictures, you will be introduced to a Lower East Side lost amidst all the gains we call progress. As Shakespeare said in "All's Well That Ends Well," "praising what is lost makes the remembrance dear." Still, it is not my intent to romanticize life in the old neighborhood. I would not want to go back to iceboxes, wood stoves, toilets on landings, or bathtubs in the kitchen, but it was home and all I knew. More importantly, it was filled with love and a sense of history and community that smoothed out the rough spots and made all the difference.

Choreography of the Streets: The Life and Work of Rebecca Lepkoff
By Suzanne Wasserman

Rebecca Lepkoff's path to becoming an internationally known photographer began on the Lower East Side, the subject of her photographs and her muse for over half a century. Lepkoff's photographs have been exhibited, published, and collected both in the United States and abroad. Life on the Lower East Side is the first published collection of her work of the neighborhood she was born in and lived in for almost fifty years.

Lepkoff (nee Brody) was born on the Lower East Side in 1916. Her parents, young newlyweds paired by a matchmaker, emigrated from Minsk in Russia in 1910. Like thousands of other eastern European Jews before them, Anna Rose Schwartz and Isadore Brody settled in a tenement apartment in New York City's teeming immigrant district. As the family grew, they moved from tenement to tenement but always stayed within a few block radius—on Hester Street, East Broadway, Clinton Street, and Jefferson Street. Rebecca's older sister, Celia, was born in 1914. Siblings Sam, William, Harry, and Pearl followed in 1918, 1920, 1925, and 1927, respectively.

The burgeoning garment industry of the turn-of-the-century Lower East Side offered plenty of work for Rebecca Lepkoff's father, who had been a skilled tailor in Russia. He worked his way up from sweatshop worker to tailor at Fisher Brothers Men's Garments on Division Street. Like many other striving immigrants, he took English classes at night after work. Lepkoff remembers, in a June 10, 2005 interview, that he "immediately became Americanized. He got a straw hat and he bought these spiffy jackets."

Despite the fact that the family of eight lived in a two-bedroom tenement apartment, Lepkoff has some happy early memories. She recalls accompanying her father to synagogue and joining the other women in the women's only balcony section and of Shabbas dinners of noodle soup and homemade gefilte fish cooked by her mother. Like many other Lower East Side fathers,

Lepkoff's father, Isadore Brody, ca. 1930

Isadore Brody was rarely home: he worked long hours to feed his family.

Unlike Lepkoff's father, her mother never adjusted to America. She resisted becoming Americanized, even refusing to learn English. After the birth of Lepkoff's youngest sister, the family's life changed forever: her mother had a nervous breakdown from which she never fully recovered. Lepkoff's mother came from a little shtetl in Russia and had led a sheltered life there as the only daughter in a family of boys. The life in the Lower East Side tenements stood in sharp contrast to her life in Russia. "She wasn't very happy," Lepkoff recalls.

> *[My mother] said that [when] everybody said that in America the streets were lined with gold...that was a big lie...To her, life in America was bitter and cold...My mother really broke down. She had a nervous breakdown and she couldn't function after a while, as a housekeeper, as a mother. And she just sort of removed herself. And my father would have hopes that she would get better, but it never happened.*

At the time of her mother's breakdown, Rebecca was about eleven years old, Celia, the oldest, only thirteen, and the youngest just an infant. As a result of her mother's condition, Celia took on many family responsibilities. In order to get a job, she applied makeup, donned high heels, and claimed she was sixteen when only thirteen. Later, she put herself through college and became an accountant. She was "very [much] like my father, just sort of grabbed a hold of American life," Rebecca recalls.

Her mother's breakdown affected the family profoundly. Rebecca Lepkoff remembers feeling helpless, confused, anxious, and worried all at once. The younger children were left to their own devices. She struggled through junior high and most of high school at Seward Park but dropped out at age sixteen, feeling stigmatized by her family's poverty despite the fact that it was the height of the Great Depression. Many Lower East Side residents, hit hard by the Depression, felt ashamed by their financial hardships.

Lepkoff's mother, Anna Rose Brody (nee Schwartz), with Lepkoff's grandmother in Russia, ca. 1910. She never adjusted to America and missed the Old Country.

I didn't have many clothes and [the teachers] would criticize what I was wearing; and they said my fingernails weren't filed right. And so, I just quit. I quit, and I didn't tell anybody. I just used to go to Seward Park Library in the morning. The whole term, I read through all the classics—all the books in the library, from eight to three o'clock. And I think I got a wonderful education that year.

Eventually, Lepkoff attended night school and received her high school diploma. "I found that I really enjoyed night school because the people were adults, and life was real. Nobody cared what you wore," Lepkoff explains.

As a teenager with no cohesive family life, Lepkoff struggled to make a life for herself. She found that she excelled in an arena that not many young women found themselves in at the beginning of the twentieth century—athletics. Without a typical disapproving mother, Lepkoff followed her brothers to the playground and learned that she was talented at sports. "I became very good as an athlete, and...Seward Park had [organized] competitions in the playground...They had races and whatnot. And I caught a couple of medals—in the 100-yard dash. I was pretty good, physically."

Her interest in athletics led her to the Educational Alliance, a settlement house and community center for immigrants opened on the Lower East Side in 1897, where Lepkoff attended gymnastics classes and participated in basketball competitions. Lepkoff vividly recalls the diversity of a basketball team she joined: "Our team had an Italian girl, an Irish girl, a Polish girl, a Jewish girl. Every nationality. And we were a winning team. But there were all different nationalities and nobody could beat us."

It was also at the Educational Alliance that she was introduced to the world of modern dance. One day, on her way up to the gym, she noticed a modern dance class occurring on a lower floor:

I passed by a room where dancers were doing different movements. I stopped to watch, and it was very interesting.

The teacher was demonstrating. And so I asked about that, and then I think I took a class there the next time. I met people who were interested in dance [at the Educational Alliance]. That's how I got involved in the dance world.

Her life choices as a young woman growing up during the Great Depression were limited. But luckily Lepkoff had found her passion and her salvation in dance. "I started to feel better when I danced," she recalls. Dancing relieved the anxiety of her troubled home life. The dance world offered an alternative to the conventional choices of early marriage (she had rejected two early proposals), or working as a bookkeeper or stenographer. Instead, Lepkoff chose the world of the artist. "I wasn't very practical," Lepkoff says.

While dancing at the Educational Alliance, she discovered Experimental Dance Group, a modern dance company led by Bill Matons, a student of the famous modern dancers Doris Humphrey and Charles Weidman. Soon, she joined Matons's company and began performing throughout New York City—in museums, union halls, and universities. She eventually taught classes for the company as well. At age twenty-one, she won a scholarship to the Doris Humphrey–Charles Weidman Dance Group. In the mid 1930s, the modern dance world was a small and exclusive one, and unfamiliar to most Americans. "If you told someone you were a modern dancer, they would say, 'What is that?'" Lepkoff recalls.

Dance opened up a new world to the young Lepkoff, seen here ca. 1932.

Still living at home, Lepkoff worked seasonally in garment industry factories, concentrating on dancing during the slow season. "I worked in a button factory. And I think another job was what they called finishing seams. Very boring work." Lepkoff's father paid the rent, gas, and electric and left his children to fend for themselves. "The family life was very thin. So you were really on your own, very much on your own," she says. But Lepkoff's life was busy and fulfilling: she worked, danced, performed, and taught dance.

Dance inadvertently led Lepkoff to photography. Following afternoon rehearsals, Lepkoff and her dance friends would visit art galleries, "go uptown to Fifty-Seventh Street, and

go to all the art galleries and look at art and photography."
She was particularly drawn to photography. During this period,
Bill Matons was asked to choreograph the 1939 World's Fair
performance about the history of railroads called Railroads on
Parade. He hired Lepkoff as one of the dancers. Everybody was
paid equity rate, and Lepkoff received a decent wage for the
first time in her life. With disposable cash in her pocket, she
bought a camera on a whim.

With the money Lepkoff earned as a dancer at the 1939 World's Fair, she bought her first camera.

With her new camera in hand, Lepkoff
decided to take advantage of free classes
in photography offered by the New Deal's
National Youth Administration. The
photography division was located in a
building in her neighborhood, at the edge of
the East River near Houston Street. Lepkoff
remembers the director of the photography
division, photographer Arnold Eagle, fondly:
"He gave me advice. He was a very encouraging
teacher—not only to me but to a lot of
people. He was a good person, a nice human
being, a good human being. And he was very interested in
the Lower East Side. He took some beautiful portraits, very
intimate portraits of faces." This respect for him further
encouraged her photographic pursuits.

It was the height of the Depression, and some of the
young people in the program, like much of the country, were
adversely affected by the economy. Nonetheless, up-and-
coming photographers gathered there, including Louis Stettner
and Louis Stoumen, "hanging out...penniless—but talented."
Lepkoff recalls that "there were times I didn't have a change
of clothes...You would wear your shoes down to nothing, and
you wouldn't be able to buy [new ones]." This was the humble
origin of Lepkoff's photography.

So that was the beginning of photography, but I was still
dancing. But that was a beginning. I was really interested
in form. It's probably an inner talent that just came about
through luck, in a way. I was very happy with the camera.

And then, able to see what I take, visual things. That
excited me right away, from the very beginning.

In 1941, Rebecca married a young man named Gene Lepkoff
she had met in dance class. Soon after, he was drafted and
served in an artillery division fighting in France and Germany
during World War II. During his absence, Rebecca moved back
in with her family. After the war, she and Gene were reunited
and moved into a cold-water flat at 343 Cherry Street. It was
somewhat of an unusual choice: other young, Jewish couples
were moving out to Long Island and New Jersey. Her memories
parallel those of Dr. Peter Dans who was born and grew up
just a few blocks from Rebecca in the neighborhood between
the bridges. Though no longer extant, the street and the
neighborhood were very much about family:

Mothers with children. People would hang out of the windows
and talk from the windows. They would sit outside and clean
the windows. You'd get photographs of that. Or they'd sit
on the fire escape when it was hot, and they'd sit on the
stoops and talk. Really, the social climate was still very
much the same as when I was little. Kind of friendly. [After
the war] there were different kinds of people that moved in,
too. There weren't only Jewish people...And I did a lot of
photography [on Cherry Street].

While many bemoaned the death of the Lower East Side
after the war, Rebecca Lepkoff was busy photographing its
life. Where others saw only change and decline, Lepkoff
captured continuity. "People ask me—how did you know what to
take? I didn't even have to think. I just went outside, and
there were the streets of my mother, of me, and whatnot. Very
alive, full of activity, with people." And in the heart of
this neighborhood, in a "sort of a railroad flat...there was a
room, a small bedroom that I made into a darkroom." Lepkoff's
life revolved more and more around photography and less around
dance. Her artistic vision transformed from choreography of the
body to the choreography of the streets around her.

In 1945, Lepkoff noticed an article in a newspaper
about the Photo League. Created in New York City in 1936 by

photographers Sid Grossman and Sol Libsohn, the Photo League
had originally been part of the Film and Photo League. The
Photo League members viewed photography as a tool for social
change and, as voiced by historian Ann Tucker, believed that
photographers should "illuminate and record the communities
in which they lived." Led by its president Walter Rosenblum,
the League ran a school, held exhibitions in its gallery,
and published a newsletter called Photo Notes. It was also
a volunteer organization open to amateurs and professionals
alike.

Leaguers were influenced by artists such as Edward Hopper
and John Sloan and by photographers such as Lewis Hine, Paul
Strand, and Alfred Stieglitz. In fact, many of these influential
photographers became active in the league, either as members
or guests: Lewis Hine directed the project Men at Work with
Photo League school students, Paul Strand taught classes, and
guest speakers included world renowned photographers Berenice
Abbott and Henri Cartier-Bresson, among others. League members
included Helen Levitt, Rudy Burckhardt, Walter Rosenblum,
Morris Engel, Arthur Leipzig, and Aaron Siskind.

Postwar New York City was, according to the writer Jan
Morris in Manhattan '45, "the future about to occur." During
this period, the visual arts flourished. By the time Lepkoff
joined the Photo League, the organization had trained hundreds
of documentary photographers. Like her contemporaries, she was
interested in the profane, the everyday, the vernacular—in
the broad, humanist outlook of fellow photographers such as
Walter Rosenblum, Helen Levitt, and Roy DeCarava. The best
possible place for encountering this material was in the
street. According to Rosenblum, leaguers "sought out scenes
that portrayed New York life as lively and affecting despite
obvious poverty." Over time, the League's goals had shifted,
as Joan Munkacsi writes, "from a social vision to a more
personal, creative one."

The activities and interests of the league intimately
paralleled Lepkoff's own; she felt right at home with the
Photo League:

The things they were doing, I found that it was close to what I was thinking about. And so, that opened up a whole era of my life in photography. I took a class with Sid Grossman, and he was a very strong teacher. Very inspiring. But some people couldn't stand him and they left because if you didn't bring in your assignment, he was very abusive. And some people weren't as serious, and they would leave. The class would start at eight o'clock, and it went on forever. And he would have his container of coffee in a paper bag and keep working, drinking it. But I did some wonderful photographs in that class, some wonderful photographs.

Grossman's instruction helped refine her photography, to be selective when printing: "Take your photograph and make proof sheets and study them. Pick out the ones that you really think are good. And when you make a print, just don't make one print. Stop when you think you have the perfect print."

During this period of her life, as a young married woman without children in postwar New York City, Lepkoff's life was consumed by photography. She had a part-time job at Haber & Fink, a well-known photography store on Warren Street in lower Manhattan. When not working, she would go out to shoot photographs:

I would always go to an area where things were happening, but I would go continuously. I would go to a certain area or street, or two or three streets where I would be interested in the buildings, or the people, or the children...And I would shoot a roll or two and then go process it and look at it, and I would go back again. So I would go back to the same place for a long time, until I felt I really got what I wanted.

Lepkoff was seemingly inexhaustible when taking photographs as well as in the darkroom. She often printed from eight o'clock in the evening until three o'clock in the morning, much to her husband's dismay. Her dedication did not separate her from her subject; her method of photographing involved making sure they felt comfortable with her:

Sometimes I would be on the street for a long time, so people would sort of feel relaxed about my being there. I have these portraits where people were just looking straight at me without posing...It's because they had seen me standing there for such a long time. There was something not scary about me. And I'd get these very intimate photographs of direct contact with my eyes, looking straight at me. I [would go back to a place] day after day. Or they would see me the week before or something. I think it helped to be a woman. They'd never think that a woman would come out with a hatchet or something like that.

Lepkoff was both sensitive to her subjects and at the same times tenacious. That she was a woman photographer made her both able to appear innocuous but also perhaps more vulnerable. She was fearless in order to get the shot she wanted, and confrontations were not infrequent. In one instance, as she was attempting to take a photograph of a facade of a building from across the street, a passer-by who was captured in the image expressed displeasure at his inclusion: "When I clicked the camera, he heard it and said, 'Give me, take the film out, give me that!'" Though I insisted that he was "only going to be like a little dot," he could not be persuaded and threatened to involve a police officer. "So we both went over to the cop. He tells the story to the cop, and the cop says, 'Listen, guy, this is a free country.' (laughing) That was the end of that."

Another instance occurred when Lepkoff was photographing in Brooklyn for a book called Street Gangs. The author, concerned about her safety, urged her to be accompanied by a police officer on location. Lepkoff addressed him, stating, "How can I take pictures with a cop in back of me?" The officer replied, "You either take the pictures or you don't take the pictures." In typical fashion, she lost sight of him. "I sat down to change my roll of film, and a man comes and says, 'What are you doing here? Somebody is going to come and break your head.' I said, 'I don't see anybody coming here to break my head. Anyhow, nothing happened to me." Lepkoff's fearlessness paid off.

In 1948, the attorney general's office listed the Photo League as a Communist-front organization, and the league was forced to close in 1951. About its demise, Lepkoff comments, "You know, there isn't any organization now that's anything like the Photo League. And if it had continued, it would have had some wonderful things come about. Because it was such a creative organization and attracted so many people—young people who had a lot of ideas. They used to take photographs of the life in America that was never photographed." Those years constituted Lepkoff's most prolific period.

Rebecca continued to photograph, but life was also consumed by the arrival of her first two children, Danny in 1950 and Jesse in 1953. After Danny's birth, the Lepkoffs left Cherry Street and moved a few blocks away to Knickerbocker Village on Madison and Monroe streets. Knickerbocker Village was a housing project that opened in 1934 to accommodate the Lower East Side's growing working white and pink-collar community. Gene had lived there with his mother and sister from 1936 to 1941 as had Dr. Dans between 1937 and 1938.

Lepkoff taught photography at the Educational Alliance, ca. 1948.

Paralleling the change in Rebecca Lepkoff's life, her photographs captured the seemingly ever-changing neighborhood of the Lower East Side. It was hard as a young mother to keep up the same pace, but her husband was supportive of her talents. She recalls one incident that signified the changes taking place. Mothers in the PTA at PS 177 on Monroe Street, like Lepkoff, protested that the textbooks at the local public schools were out-of-date and wanted to account for the newly migrated Puerto Rican children in the schools who did not speak English.

The PTAs were very active with the women that lived in Knickerbocker Village because there were a lot of intelligent young mothers. We wanted to get the Puerto Rican mothers to come, so we kept on sending out announcements saying that we were going to have a party, a special celebration. Nobody came, until—we don't know why—someone, somebody who knew the Puerto Rican people said, "The women

*don't go out at night." So we planned to have an afternoon
thing, and they came...all with their beautiful colors, with
the flowers. My photographs are about the life of people at
that time, at that particular time. And it's the time where
these particular activities were important in their lives,
and important in the lives of America.*

After Lepkoff's daughter, Tamar, was born in 1962,
her husband convinced her to move the family to a house in
Teaneck, New Jersey. "I didn't want to leave the city,"
Lepkoff recalls. In an ironic twist, Lepkoff missed the dirty,
messy streets of the Lower East Side as much as her mother had
missed the country and the openness of her little village in
Russia. As soon as their children were grown, Lepkoff and her
husband moved back to the city in 1979. She has photographed
New York City for sixty-six years, lending her unique eye to a
familiar neighborhood.

*I think photographers today should really look around and
think of what they are seeing. They should just think about
the meaning of what they are looking at. That is, to drink
it in. People just walk through the streets and just see
things, and if you ask them a little later on, "What did you
see?" I don't know if you're going to get much of an answer...
I think that if a photographer has a camera, he or she has
to think of what's out there and make a statement. It has
nothing to do with the camera, really. It has to do with the
way they see life. The camera is visual. But they have to
know what they are thinking and feeling...If you walk around
the streets and you don't really see, in a thinking way,
what's out there—then it's useless.*

Rebecca Lepkoff has exhibited her photographs at the
International Center of Photography, The New York Public
Library, Fourteenth Street YMHA, Pfeifer Gallery, Daniel
Wolf Gallery, Howard Greenberg Gallery, and Henry Street
Settlement. Her work is in the permanent collections of the
National Gallery of Art in Washington, D.C., National Gallery
of Canada, and Bank of America, among others. Her photographs

appear in *A History of Women Photographers* by Naomi Rosenblum, *Bystander: A History of Street Photography* by Joel Meyerowitz and Colin Westerbeck, and *Street Gangs* by Sandra Gardiner. She is represented by the prestigious Howard Greenberg Gallery in New York City and still lives in New York City with her husband.

Plates

Cherry Street

Cherry Street was named for a Dutch merchant's orchard that yielded the best cherries in town in the 1660s. It began at Franklin Square, in a hill that once housed a number of illustrious citizens, including Washington and Hancock, and ran to Corlear's Hook just past Jackson Street. In the 1850s, Gotham Court on Cherry Hill, which had started as a model tenement, was labeled one of the worst tenements along the East River. The site of bawdy houses, gangs, and violence, Cherry and Water Streets were where the "swells" went slumming until the turn of the century. By the 1930s, many of the old law tenements had either been modernized or razed. Cherry Street was a stable blue-collar neighborhood of Italians, Irish, Jewish, and Spanish immigrants.

"The Sicilian downstairs put out the tomato sauce to bake in the sun—and the Irish upstairs hung up her clothes...When she took off the clothespins...sometimes the pillow case, went in the sauce. Then they both got mad and stated fighting."

From *Rosa: The Life of an Italian Immigrant* by Marie Hall Ets

opposite: Fresh fruit and vegetables were only available to most residents of the Lower East Side during the summer. As they drove their horse and wagons, vendors would shout "Wateemellones [*sic*] red like fire, sweet like sugar!" On James Slip between Water and South streets, there was a big horse trough where vendors and horses could rest and refresh.

The "Welcome Boys" sign is a poignant
reminder that many of the neighborhood men
served in World War II and of the pride
and happiness experienced by the residents
upon their return.

Peddling proliferated on the Lower East Side because it provided work for its residents, especially during hard times, as well as a cheap, familiar, and efficient place for residents to shop.

Many long-term residents had lived for years in the same apartment
buildings with their family and friends. But in the mid-1930s, many
tenements were condemned and razed as a part of a much-anticipated
housing reform movement. Rather than leave the neighborhood upon
eviction, they moved to nearby buildings together and continued
to live as a close-knit community. Although some adequate public
housing arose, most living conditions on the Lower East Side
continued to be substandard throughout the 1940s.

Robert Caro in *The Power Broker* writes,
"Robert Moses tore out the hearts of
a score of neighborhoods, communities
the size of small cities themselves,
communities that had been lively, friendly
places to live, the vital parts of the city
that made New York a home to its people."

63

The Taylor's home at 343 Cherry Street
documents the slum conditions of the area.
The Taylors exude closeness and dignity
despite continued deleterious housing
conditions.

Beginning on December 26, 1947, and
continuing through the next day, 25.8
inches of snow fell on New York City, its
largest snowfall until 2006. Popularly
called the "blizzard of 1947," even though
the winds were not strong enough for it to
qualify as such, it paralyzed the city for
days. City dwellers coped with equanimity
and even fun during the aftermath.

Early reformers saw street life as a reflection of apathy and leisure. Why were women sitting on the stoop and standing on street corners idly chatting instead of staying inside their homes? But on the Lower East Side, the street and the stoop were extensions of tenement living rooms. Children played on the stoop under the watchful eyes of parents and grandparents and neighbors.

71

The Waterfront: Fulton Street Fish Market and South Street

South Street replaced Water Street, after much infilling, as the water's edge of the East River and was dotted with many ferry slips. South Street was best known as the home of the Fulton Fish market, which began as a few fish stalls in the Fulton Market in 1822. Between midnight and 9:00 a.m., it was bustling with buyers and workers. Across from the market were Sloppy Louie's Restaurant, renowned for its bouillabaisse, and the Fulton Ferry Hotel, made famous by *New Yorker* writer Joseph Mitchell, in his essay "Up at the Old Hotel." The grit, noise, and orchestrated chaos of the market ceased in 2005 when it moved to Hunt's Point.

"A Puerto Rican man who had come to New York in the 1950s recently told the journalist
Robert Suro: 'I started after school hauling ice, and then as soon as I was sixteen,
I dropped out of school and went down to the Fulton Street docks to become a stevedore.
When there was no work at the docks, you could always go to the garment district and
look for signs...and I never spent a day on relief.'"
From "New York, New York: The Life and Times of Gotham, the City by the Sea" by Fred Siegel

84

84

84

Essex and Delancey Streets

Delancey Street has traditionally been the Lower East Side's main traffic artery and shopping district. The indoor Essex Street Market, created to remove peddlers from the streets, officially opened in January of 1940. Never entirely successful, the indoor market did not have the ambience of the streets. During the 1930s, fifteen thousand peddlers lined the streets. By 1945, only twelve hundred remained. For slightly upscale shopping, Lower East Siders traveled uptown to Fourteenth Street and shopped at Klein's on the Square and Orhbach's.

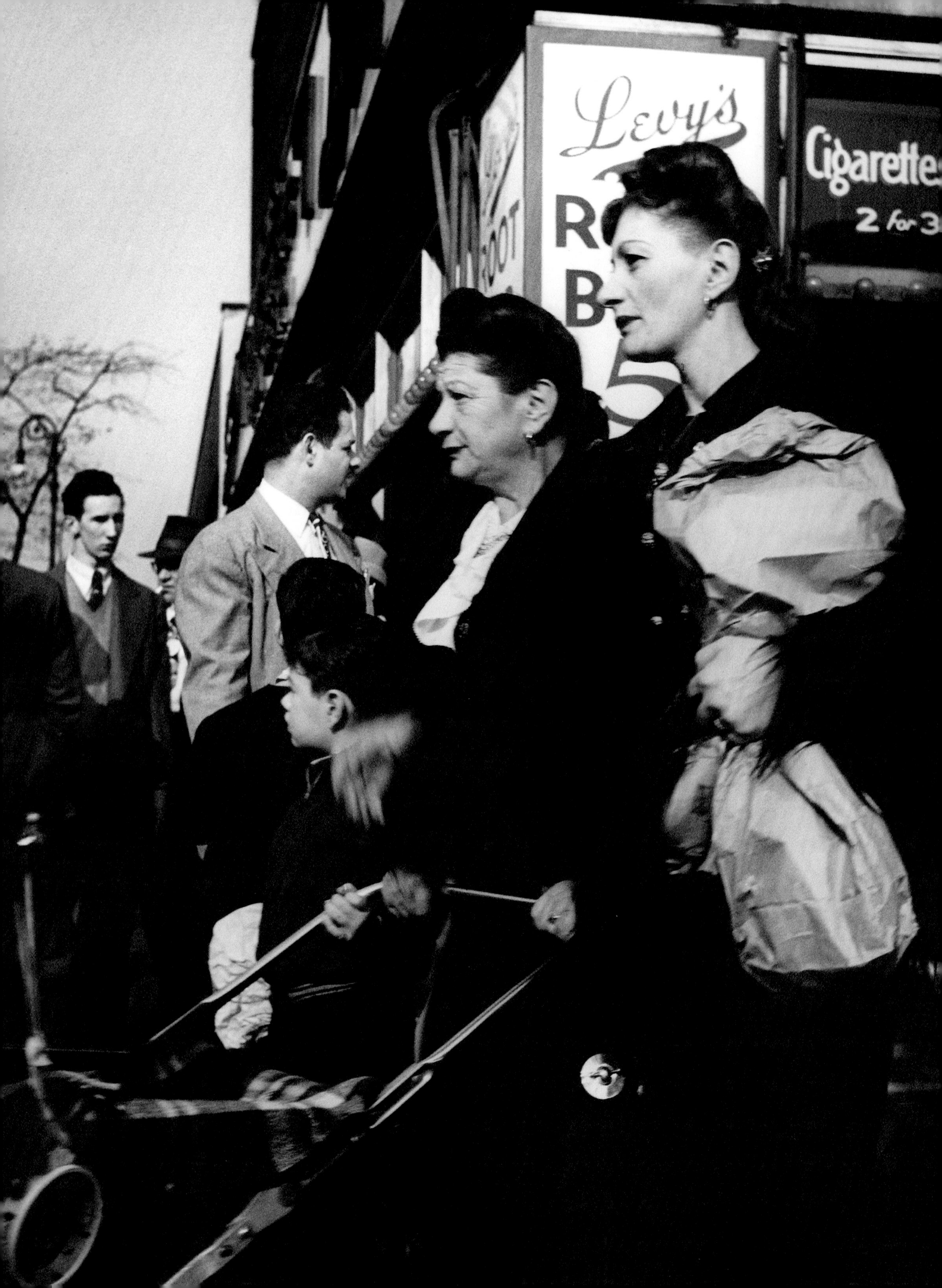
Levy's
ROOT
R
B
5
Cigarettes
2 for 3

In March 1947, a visitor from Mexico died
of smallpox after a week of sightseeing in
the city. The last smallpox epidemic had
occurred in 1902, making the disease less
recognizable to doctors during the man's
visit to two hospitals. At a third hospital
where he eventually died, two more patients
contracted the disease and a diagnosis
was made, which led to a massive free
vaccination campaign that reached over six
million New Yorkers in a single month. As
a result, only eleven cases were recorded,
and there were no additional deaths.

Fourteenth Street was the place to go for
special shopping—at S. Klein's on the
Square, Ohrbach's, Lane's, fur stores, and
myriad other good value outlets. Shoppers
also had a wide choice of eateries ranging
from Milk Bars selling Charlotte Russes,
a restaurant featuring chop suey, the
Automat, to the world-famous Luchow's,
which closed on its hundredth anniversary
in 1982.

Rooftop tanks made of yellow cedar or
redwood and girdled by steel hoops became
part of the city skyline in the 1880s
when buildings began to top six stories
and the existing city water pressure was
insufficient to reach the upper floors. Water
was pumped into the tanks, which served as
gravity-operated reservoirs. Now they are
mainly quaint reminders of an earlier time.

East Broadway and Henry Street

East Broadway and Henry Street were the heart of the Jewish Lower East Side. On East Broadway is the esteemed Jewish Daily Forward Building erected in 1897. At the time, it was the tallest building on the Lower East Side and boasted the largest circulation of any Yiddish daily newspaper in the world. Two important settlements—Educational Alliance and Henry Street Settlement were also located in this area. In 1893, Lillian Wald opened The Henry Street Settlement and worked tirelessly for improvements in health, education, housing, and recreation for the neighborhood.

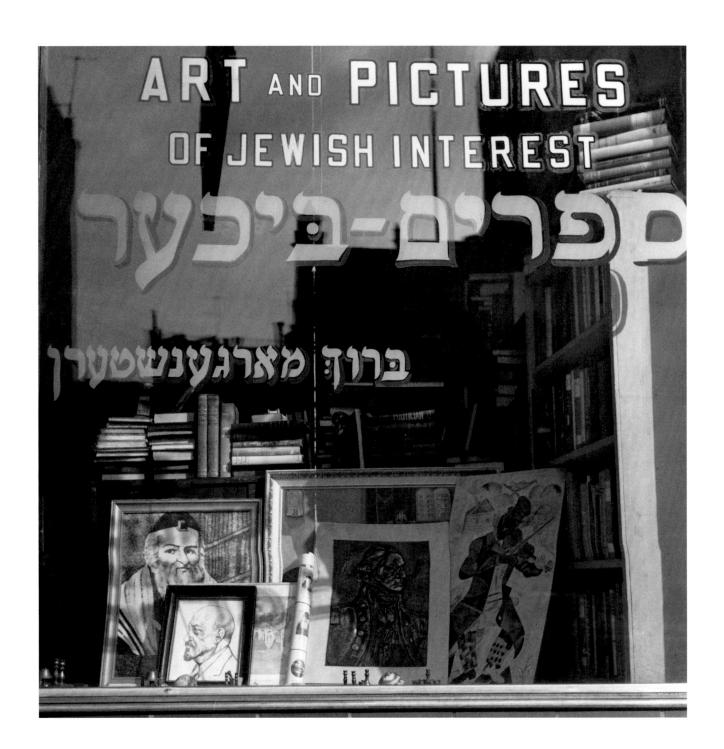

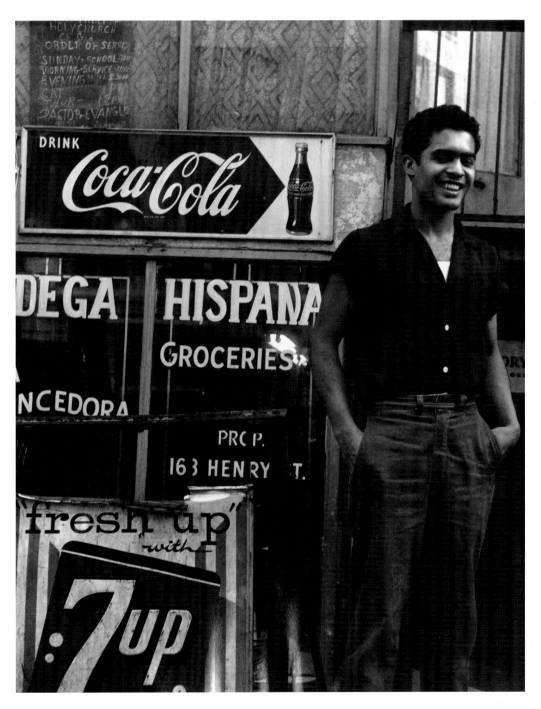

During these years, this neighborhood was an early area of
settlement for migrating Puerto Ricans and African Americans.
Between 1940 and 1950, the combined Latino and Black population on
the Lower East Side grew from 4,500 to over 12,000. By 1957,
it had doubled again. The first airborne migration brought a half
million Puerto Ricans to New York City by 1955, many of whom settled
on the Lower East Side.

Among social critics during the 1930s, the most talked about and debated form of leisure time activities by far was the movies, especially in regards to children. Many children went to the neighborhood movie houses up to three times a week. Young people with a bit more pocket change went as often as six times a week.

More popular than commercialized venues—like pool halls, dance halls, and the movies—the streets were the overwhelming first choice for leisure-time activities for children, young men and women, parents, and grandparents. Stoops, rooftops, fire escapes, and storefronts were the predominant leisure settings for family sociability and relaxation and remained so throughout the 1940s.

Hester and Suffolk

Hester Street was the traditional site of the main open-air pushcart market in the Lower East Side. In 1886, four peddlers planted pushcarts on Hester Street. Considered the first documented stationary pushcart market in New York City, the vendors immediately did brisk business with local customers, selling everything from fruit, vegetables, bread, hot knishes, bagel, hot *arbis* (boiled chick peas) to tools and used clothing. During the 1930s, these streets were transformed when the LaGuardia administration removed peddlers from the streets as of December 1, 1938 and relocated them to indoor markets.

"The East Side takes its pushcart so
seriously that you are greatly impressed
with it, when you go down there and see
and hear the hundreds of men engaged in
the actual selling and pushing...In other
parts of the town the pushcart is a mere
incident...but within that precinct he has
distinct place and finding."
From "The Pushcart Peddlers" by Olive Gundy

Pickles used to be sold on the Lower East Side of New York from wooden pickle barrels at stationary stoop line stands for a penny a pickle. Families who owned pickle stands often made their own pickles. Harry Baker, of Gus's Pickles, once told a reporter that he got annoyed when customers waxed nostalgic for the old wooden barrels: "Wood barrels are a myth. I couldn't wait to get rid of them and get plastic. The wood ones leak and hold bacteria. Plastic actually ages the pickles better!"

Opened in 1934, Knickerbocker Village was the first major private housing complex
to receive public funds. It replaced the once notorious nineteenth-century slum on
Hamilton Street called the "Lung Block," for having the highest tuberculosis rate in
the city. Displacing hundreds of mostly Italian families, it accommodated thousands
of middle-class residents in twelve-story buildings, which developer Fred F. French
proudly declared were "outfitted with General Electric refrigerators, Otis elevators
and Standard sanitary fixtures." This panoramic view was taken from the roof of
Knickerbocker Village.

Madison, Oak, and Monroe Streets

The area encompassed by Madison, Monroe,
and South streets including Oak,
Roosevelt, James, and Oliver streets—
largely demolished to build the Al
Smith housing project—always attracted
immigrant populations. It was once the
hub of a substantial Greek community and
a strong Irish enclave, Tammany Hall's
ever-reliable Fourth Ward. By the early
twentieth century, Italian and Jewish
immigrants settled in large numbers, and
the neighborhood took on the flavor and
character of their respective cultures.
Now Chinese, Latino, and African-American
influences abound.

During the 1930s and 1940s, the five square blocks of the Lower East
Side between the bridges continued to be heavily immigrant: Jewish,
Italian, Irish, Greeks, and Spaniards. More importantly, it was an
area of resistance to Americanization. Many of these Lower East Side
residents were still non-citizens, although most had been in America
at least two decades. Over half spoke a foreign language exclusively
at home. Their vibrant and close-knit community defied contemporary
descriptions of the neighborhood as a "slum," a locus of broken
dreams, delinquency, decline, and personal failure.

Until the mid-nineteenth century in New York City, meat and
vegetables could only be sold in public markets. This allowed for
control and inspection of meat. Butchers paid a tax for the exclusive
right to sell in the markets. Butchers, who wore high hats and long
tailed coats, were the aristocrats of the early markets. But in
1841, butchers began selling meat from shops. Merchant folklore has
it that the first butcher was fined $100, but the public preferred the
shops. Thereafter, shops reigned. This twentieth century butcher
retains the aura of aristocracy from the earlier era.

Although Mayor Fiorello LaGuardia had officially banned pushcart peddling by 1938, it persisted. He had succeeded in changing the face of the streets. Before his election in 1934, there were 15,000 peddlers in the city. By 1945, only 1,200 had legal licenses to peddle, many on the Lower East Side.

Adults, and sometimes their children, congregated in cafes, coffeehouses and wine cellars. During this period, many former Lower East Sider residents began returning to the Lower East Side because they missed the smells, sights, and sounds of their pasts. Merchants catered to their nostalgic longings by creating synthetic, re-creations of Lower East Side restaurants and cabarets. A *Saturday Evening Post* article entitled "East Side Cafes," warned visitors away from establishments south of Houston Street frequented by the "natives." They warned that the establishments were in dangerous areas and frequented by dangerous sorts of people.

"The great army of
barbers, bootblacks,
fruiterers, and
shoemakers in our
cities and towns...are
from cities and small
towns in Italy...Their
business success is
notable and they have
brought their trades
generally to a higher
level than that in which
they found them...
The Italian shoemaker
lags behind in this
list, being of the old-
fashioned cobbler type."
From "The Foreign Immigrant
in New York City," *Reports
of the Industrial Commission
volume xv, 1901* by Kate
Holladay Claghorn, Ph.D.

174

In the days before television, the almost one thousand movie houses provided New Yorkers with escape from everyday life and a temporary air conditioned relief from the stifling summer heat. Movie openings at first-run uptown theaters like the Paramount, the Capitol, and the Mayfair were heralded on neighborhood fences that also served to hide the rubble of the empty lots where building demolition had already begun.

The area of the Lower East Side between Fulton
Street and the Manhattan Bridge was once served
by two police precincts, the First Precinct at
Old Slip (now The New York Police Department
Museum) and the Third Precinct on Oak Street.
The Third precinct no longer exists having been
supplanted by One Police Plaza.

The nearby junction of Park Row and
Pearl Street was the site of a little-
known milestone in racial progress.
Elizabeth Jennings, an African-American
schoolteacher and forerunner of Rosa
Parks, boarded a trolley reserved for
whites in 1854 one Sunday on her way to
play the organ in a church at Second
Avenue and Sixth Street. Her forcible
removal led to publicity, community
activism, and aid from Frederick
Douglass and a young lawyer and future
president Chester Alan Arthur. The
victory in her legal challenge led to
the desegregation of New York City
streetcars.

The Third Avenue El and Chatham Square

The Third Avenue Elevated Line, "The El," opened in 1878 and eventually connected the Battery to the Bronx along Pearl Street, the Bowery, and Third Avenue. At Chatham Square station, a portion of the line split off to end at Brooklyn Bridge and City Hall and the remainder continued to South Ferry. The El was the stuff of legend, forever darkening the Bowery, which was regaled in song and stories as a place where vice and the homeless found shelter in its shadows. It was a favorite location shot for 1940s noir films such as *The Lost Weekend*, *A Double Life*, and *The Naked City*. The City Hall spur was discontinued in 1944, and the last El train ran in 1955 when the line and its stations were dismantled.

Italian feasts were held in streets in association with nearby churches beginning in
the 1880s. Meant to honor a patron saint and to recall the old country, they consisted
of traditional customs such as carrying of the saint's or Madonna's statue and the
posting of money on to the statue with requests for favors as well as eating, games,
and singing. Every August, electric lights were erected over now-extinct streets,
such as Oak, Roosevelt, and New Chambers, to celebrate the Feast of Saint Rocco, in
conjunction with nearby St. Joachim's Church where Mother Cabrini, the first U.S.
citizen to be recognized as a saint by the Roman Catholic Church, began her American
ministry.

The circus is gone and so is the neighborhood.

As almost every commentator on New York has
noted, the city is about change and survival.
E. B. White stated it poetically in "Here is
New York," comparing the city to a willow
tree: "It is a battered tree, long-suffering
and much-climbed, held together by strands
of wire but beloved of those who know it. In
a way, it symbolizes the city: life under
difficulties, growth against odds, sap rise
in the midst of concrete, and the steady
reaching for the sun."

Selected Bibliography

Bunyan, Patrick. *All Around the Town: Amazing Manhattan Facts and Curiosities*. New York: Fordham University Press, 1999.

Burns, Ric and James Sanders, with Ades Lisa. *New York: An Illustrated History*. New York: Alfred A. Knopf, 1999.

Caro, Robert. *The Power Broker: Robert Moses and the Fall of New York*. New York: Vintage Books, 1974.

Creative Camera. *The Photo League* 223 and 224 (July/August 1983).

Ets, Marie Hall. *Rosa: The Life of an Italian Immigrant* Minneapolis: University of Minnesota Press, 1970.

Federal Writers' Project. *The WPA Guide to New York City*. New York: Pantheon, 1982. First published in 1939 by Guild Committee for Federal Writers Publications Inc.

Gold, Michael. *Jews without Money*. New York: Avon, 1965. First published in 1930 by Horace Liveright Press.

Gunby, Olive. "The Pushcart Peddlers, The Swarms in and About Hester Street." *New York Evening Post*, August 20, 1898.

Kannapell, Andrea, Jesse McKinley, Daniel B. Schneider, Kathryn Shattuck, and Jennifer Steinhauer. *The Curious New Yorker: 329 Fascinating Questions and Surprising Answers About New York City*. New York: Times Books Random House, 1999.

Lockwood, Charles. *Manhattan Moves Uptown*. Boston: Houghton Mifflin, 1976.

Lopate, Phillip. *Waterfront: A Journey Around Manhattan*. New York: Crown Publishers 2004.

Mitchell, Joseph. *Up in the Old Hotel*. New York: Vintage, 1993. First published in 1992 by Pantheon.

Morris, Jan. *Manhattan '45*. New York: Oxford University Press, 1986.

Moscow, Henry. *The Street Book: An Encyclopedia of Manhattan's Street Names and Their Origins*. New York: Fordham University Press, 1978.

Moses, Robert. "Slums and City Planning." *Atlantic Monthly*,

January 1945, 63–68.

Munkacsi, Joan. *The Photo League 1936–1951*. New York: Howard
     Greenberg/Photofind Gallery, 1985.

O'Donnell, Edward T. "Church of the Transfiguration." In *The
     Encyclopedia of New York City*, edited by Kenneth T.
     Jackson, 224. New Haven: Yale University Press, 1995.

Reynolds, Donald M. *Architecture of New York City*. New York:
     MacMillan, 1984.

Siegel, Fred. "New York, New York: The Life and Times of
     Gotham, the City by the Sea. *The Weekly Standard*,
     February 8, 1999, 39.

Simon, Kate. *New York Places and Pleasures*. New York: Meridian
     Books, 1959.

Stern, Robert A. M., Thomas Mellins, and David Fishman. *New
     York 1880*. New York: Monacelli Press, 1999.

Stetler, Lawrence. *By the El: Third Avenue and its El at Mid-
     Century*. Flushing, NY: H&M Productions. 1995.

Tucker, Anne. *The Photo League 1936–1951*. New York: Photofind
     Gallery, n.d.

Walsh, Kevin. "Street Necrology." Forgotten New York. http://
     www.forgotten-ny.com.

Wasserman, Suzanne. "The Good Old Days of Poverty: The Battle
     over the Fate of New York City's Lower East Side during
     the Depression." PhD diss., New York University, 1990.

Watson, Edward B. and Edmund V. Gillon, Jr. *New York Then and
     Now*. New York: Dover Publications, 1978.

White, E. B. *Here is New York*. New York: The Little Bookroom,
     1999.

Whitehead, Colson. *The Colossus of New York: A City in 13
     Parts*. New York: Doubleday, 2003.

A graduate of Manhattan College and Columbia University
College of Physicians and Surgeons, **Peter E. Dans** is currently
an associate professor of medicine at Johns Hopkins University
and works on issues related to drug safety in the elderly. He
is the author of a book about the portrayal of doctors in film
titled *Doctors in the Movies: Boil the Water and Just Say Aah!*
(Medi-Ed Press, 2000) and a children's book about the urban
nesting of peregrine falcons, *Perry's Baltimore Adventure: A
Birds-eye View of Charm City (Tidewater Publishers, 2003).*

Suzanne Wasserman is an historian and award-winning filmmaker.
She has a Ph.D. in American History from New York University.
She is the associate director of the Gotham Center for New
York City History at the City University of New York, Graduate
Center. She was an historical consultant on Ron Howard's film
Cinderella Man.